SIGN LANGUAGE
FOR CHILDREN

Children's Reading & Writing Education Books

Baby iQ
Builder Books
EDUCATIONAL BOOKS FOR KIDS

Sign Language Alphabet

Aa

Bb

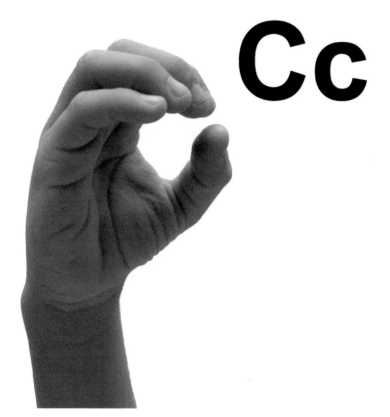

Cc

Dd

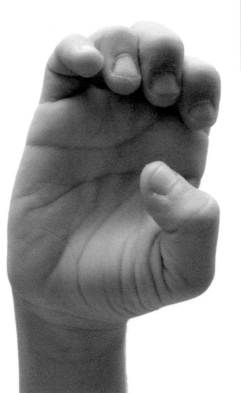

Ee

Ff

Gg

Hh

Ii

J j

Kk

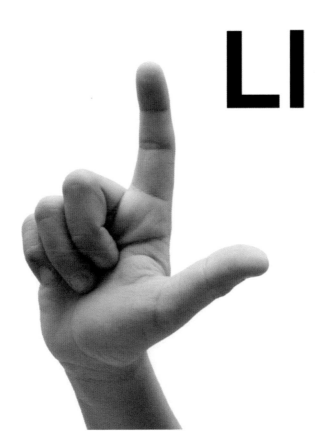

Ll

Mm

Nn

Oo

Pp

Qq

Rr

Ss

Tt

Uu

Vv

Ww

Xx

Yy

Zz

1

2

3

4

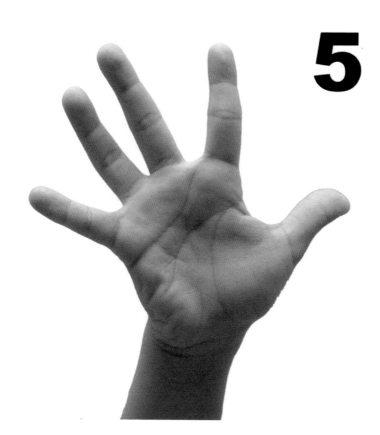

5

6

7

8

9

10

Printed in Great Britain
by Amazon